Dion Fortune's
Book of the Dead

Dion Fortune's
Book of the Dead

Dion Fortune

WEISERBOOKS
Boston, MA/York Beach, ME

This edition first published in 2005 by
Red Wheel/Weiser, LLC
York Beach, ME
With offices at:
368 Congress Street
Boston, MA 02210
www.redwheelweiser.com

The Library of Congress has catalogued the original paperback edition as follows: 99-053446

ISBN 1-57863-336-2

Typeset in AGaramond 12/15 by Garrett Brown

Printed in Canada

TCP

12 11 10 09 08 07 06 05
 8 7 6 5 4 3 2 1

Contents

Introduction

D ion Fortune originally published this book as *Through the Gates of Death*, in 1930. In the seventy odd years since Fortune's book first came out, attitudes toward death have changed considerably and not at all. Much has been written about the meaning and ritual practices of death. We tend to know more medically and spiritually about it. But by in large, we still leave death up to the experts—the death of loved ones as well as our own.

In her 1963 exposé, *The American Way of Death*, Jessica Mitford charged the North American death-care industry with preying on the grief, guilt, remorse, and confusion of the newly bereaved through the production of lavish sham rituals "where the trappings of Gracious Living are transformed, as in a nightmare, into the trappings of Gracious Dying." Coffins become "sleep chambers," hearses are "coaches," flowers are "floral tributes," corpses are "loved ones," cremated ashes are "cremains," "grief therapy" is provided for, and the psychological importance of the "memory picture"—the last glimpse of the deceased in an open casket—is stressed. "No law requires embalming. . . . The purpose of embalming is to make the corpse presentable for viewing in a suitably costly container."

Mitford found the American funeral to be in the service of nothing so much as the death-care industry's limitless drive for profit. That drive has gone largely unimpeded because of our tendency to approach the reality of death by mostly wishing it would go away. By remaining ignorant of what to do and how to behave, of what's expected, what's appropriate, what's even legal and/or necessary when someone we love dies, we leave ourselves wide open to the sweet-talking fraud and final bill of the so-called expert.

We let them handle it because we do not want to face it.

Mitford's book resulted in legislation getting passed and certain practices being shaved back by funeral sellers, but thirty-five years later, in *The American Way of Death Revisited*, Mitford reported that a simple cremation can now cost you $1000 and that the death-care industry is securely in the hands of multinational corporations.

Because we still do not want to face it.

Psychiatrist Elisabeth Kubler-Ross took on the death taboo with a book she wrote in defiance of what she recognized as our widespread denial of death. In *On Death and Dying*, she interviewed hundreds of patients diagnosed with terminal diseases. This was in the sixties, when the truth about patient diagnoses was still routinely being kept from both patients and their families. She asked why this was so. Was it for the mental well-being of the patient? Of the family? Or because some doctors had problems of their own with the realities of death?

"We're all terminal; it's just a matter of timing," goes the joke. Life ends. We know that. But what happens next? Theories vary. Western religions teach of an afterlife—heaven, purgatory, hell. Eastern religions have another take. Near the end of the seventies, when Kubler-Ross got interested in mysticism and spirituality, she came to wonder out loud if death existed at all, if maybe the dying didn't simply pass from one world into another.

At about the same time, Raymond Moody, Jr. published *Life After Life*, an exploration of the similarities he found in the stories of those who "died and came back." According to Moody, the accounts of Near Death Experiences all share at least twelve out of fifteen elements—the noise, the tunnel, the others, a being of light, a life review, the crossing of a border/line/limit/door/ditch, after which there can be no turning back. The commonality of these and nine other features led to the coinage of a New Age acronym NDE, which, mistakenly or not, has come to stand for the promise of a continuity of consciousness from life into death.

So, we've come some distance in our understanding of life and death, but still most of us will end up dying isolated in hospital beds, too doped up on medication to notice when our consciousness shifts from this world into the next, if that's what happens. We'll never know.

Why? Because we still leave death up to the so-called experts. Why? Because we are afraid. Is there anything to be afraid of?

Dion Fortune says no.

In fact, she says that to become aware of what happens at death is not only an opportunity to improve the transition for ourselves and for our loved ones, it is the responsibility of the living to the dying at the time of death to understand the process the soul is going through in order to help. How can we know how to help if we don't know what they are going through? Why, if we know what they are going through, would we not want to help?

There is nothing to be afraid of. It's that simple. *Dion Fortune's Book of the Dead* is a guidebook as surely as is *The Egyptian Book of the Dead* or *The Tibetan Book of the Dead*. It's purpose is the same. In these pages you'll discover what happens at the time of death, what you can do, what you needn't/shouldn't do. In simple steps, Fortune teaches us how best to help facilitate the changes that the soul goes through at death. Our job as the living is to help the soul of the dying make a smooth transition.

Fortune shows how certain traditional customs connected with the passing of a soul have their roots in what she calls psychic fact. The custom of placing candles and fresh flowers in the death chamber as soon as the soul has departed, for instance, is based on the fact that "there is a brief interregnum between the disanimation of the physical body and the withdrawal of the soul from the etheric double" during which the soul remains close to the physical body, "gradually disentangling itself from the meshes of matter and reorienting itself to its new state."

Thus cut off from its supply of prana or etheric vitality, the etheric body will draw this vitality from whatever source is available—including grievers. Loved ones in particular are susceptible to this form of depletion and can be drained dry in their ignorance. But the unguarded flame of a burning candle and a vase of fresh flowers in the room will supply enough etheric emanations to meet the needs of the etheric double.

It is a simple thing to place flowers and candles in the room and it makes the transition easier for everyone. Flowers aren't just "floral tributes"; they serve a purpose. Think of all the plastic roses strewn about our cemeteries appearing to be or standing for something we have long ago lost touch with. These are lies and testimony to our spiritual estrangement.

Ultimately, the living have two tasks to perform:

1. "We must see to it that dust returns to dust as swiftly and harmoniously as possible, giving rise to none of those happenings which may be termed the pathologies of death."

2. "We ought to follow up the departing soul with the right kind of telepathic communication until it is safely established on the Other Side."

This second point reveals the purpose of prayer. Prayer is not an idle exercise or something done by rote because it's called for on the program at the funeral service. It, too, serves a purpose in helping souls make the transition.

Dion Fortune was one of the twentieth century's most significant figures of esoteric thought. She was a prolific writer, a pioneer psychologist, and a powerful psychic. So, in a way she is yet another expert. But what she does with her expertise in this book enables us to become experts at taking care of our loved ones and preparing for our own death.

She grounds us in the truth of what death is. She steers our focus forward toward what is required of us given what is actually taking place. We needn't seek to escape in self-serving sorrow and despair. We can reclaim our knowledge of what death is and what death asks of us. We needn't let the experts handle this. We are the experts. We can remember or relearn what we once knew and then forgot. Dion Fortune tells us how in her elegant, upright, slightly dated prose. We can remember to think of our lives and our deaths as

> rising and falling like a boat on the crest of a wave. Now descending into matter through the gates at birth; now re-ascending to the invisible world through the gates of death . . . as one shore fades, the further one begins to rise above the skyline . . . thoughts of love, not grief, follow that soul upon its journey, as sea-gulls follow a ship . . . sending forth our thoughts like birds into the Unseen . . . waters parting at the prow of a boat . . . a purling brook . . .

This volume is a treasure, full of wisdom and warmth and spiritual instruction.

—Gary Leon Hill,
author of *People Who Don't Know They're Dead*

1
The Great Anaesthetist

Death is a universal experience. No one can hope to escape. It is only a matter of time till it comes to each one of us and each one of those we love. Yet Death is called the King of Terrors and is the supreme threat of the law to the wrong-doer, what is it that makes a natural process so terrible ? Is it the pain of dying? No, for painkillers can deaden that. Most death-beds are peaceful when the time comes and few souls go out struggling. What, then, is it we fear in death that it should be for us a thing of grief and dread?

Firstly; we fear the Unknown.
For in that sleep of death what dreams may come
When we have shuffled of this mortal coil?

Secondly, we dread the separation from those we love. These are the things which make death terrible. How differently should we set out to cross the Threshold were our minds at rest on these two points.

It is recorded that the great gift of the Greek Mysteries to their initiates was release from the fear of death. It is said that no initiate ever fears death. What was it that was taught in those secret rites that robbed death of its terrors?

In the centre of the Great Pyramid of Gizeh there is an empty stone coffin. Egyptologists tell us that it was prepared for a Pharaoh who never occupied it. It has also been said that it was a measure for corn. It was neither of these things, but the altar of the Chamber of Initiation. In it lay the candidate while his soul was sent out upon the journey of death and recalled, and this constituted the supreme degree of the Mysteries. After that experience he never feared death again. He knew what it was. It is the knowledge guarded in the Mysteries which I propose to reveal in these pages. Death, for the man who has this knowledge, is like the embarkation of the rich man upon a liner. He is educated, he knows where he is going, he acquiesces in the journey, realising its necessity and advantages. His knowledge and resources enable him to travel in comfort and safety. He can keep in touch with his friends at will, and return to them when he desires. For him there is no final and complete severance from his native land.

Far otherwise is it with the poor peasant emigrant. Ignorant and helpless, the journey to him is a dangerous and hazardous under-taking and the land of his sojourn may be filled with wild beasts or undermined with volcanic fires. His ignorant imagination pictures all the terrors he can conceive and applies them to the Unknown.

The ancient Egyptians placed in every coffin a so-called Book of the Dead, the ritual of Osiris in the Underworld, which instructed the soul concerning its journey through the kingdoms of the shades. It might more truly be called the Book of the Ever-living, for the soul was conceived of as going through certain stages in that cycle of life which takes place in the Unseen.

It would be well for us were we taught from our earliest years to think of our lives as rising and falling like a boat on the crest of a wave. Now descending into matter through the gates of birth; now re-ascending to the invisible world through the gates of death, ever and anon to return again and withdraw again in the rhythmical cyclic tide of evolving life.

Uninstructed by the Mysteries, our lives are bounded by the horror of birth and the terror of death. How great is the gift of the guarded wisdom which reveals the road of evolving life stretching before our feet and robs the Unseen of its shadows.

Let us cease to think of Death as the Fury with the abhorred shears and conceive of it as the Great Anaesthetist, bidden by the mercy of God to cause a deep sleep to fall upon us while the silver cord is loosed and the soul set free.

From that sleep we awake refreshed, with the problems of earth far behind us, like a young child's memories of the previous day, and embark upon a fresh phase of our existence. Well is it for us if our friends give us quittance and permit the soul to go to its own place . Ill is it for us if the grief of those we have left behind shadows that bright morning waking. Just as we feel that we have the right to ask for tendence in our sickness from those who are kin to us, so should we feel that we have the right to ask of them fortitude in their bereavement.

For it is their bereavement, not ours. Whom do we grieve for when we mourn at a funeral? For the Ever-living Dead, in their bright awakening? Or for ourselves in our loneliness? Assuredly we grieve for no one but ourselves, for it is well with the dead: they have gone to their own place and are at peace.

It is those who are left behind who are suffering, not those who have gone before us into Galilee. And what shall we say concerning their suffering? That like all pain, it must be bravely borne, and especially so in this case, for its reverberations may affect others as well as ourselves, and be as a mill-stone about the neck of the soul that is seeking to rise up on the strong wings of aspiration. Let thoughts of love, not grief, follow that soul upon its journey, as sea-gulls follow a ship. Let us bid him God-speed and good cheer, and look forward to the reunion.

For there is much we can do for the departed. Our work is not finished when the coffin is borne from the house and we have put away the sad paraphernalia of illness. If they know more than we do of the ancient, guarded, secret Wisdom, it may well be that they will return to comfort us and give us good counsel. But if we know more than they do, if the soul has gone out in bewilderment and fear, or if it be that of a young child, then it is our bounden duty to follow it out into the Unseen as far as lies in our power, until we feel the coming of the Angels (of which more shall be said later), and know that our loved one has passed into their care and all is well.

And there may come to us if we ask, that Angel which giveth the beloved sleep, the deep sleep which is well known to fall upon the watchers of the dead and which is like no other sleep; and from that sleep we too should awaken to the morning calm, for it has been permitted to us to look through the gates ajar and see that beyond the Threshold there is neither terror nor oblivion, but another world, another phase of life.

Out of this sleep which the Angel of Death giveth to the beloved there cometh security and assurance; for we have seen, even if we do not remember. Let us therefore, when the hour is over, ask of the Great Anaesthetist this lesser mercy that we may be tided over the first wrench of the separation and be the better enabled to take up the burden of life and do our duty to those loved ones that are left to us, depending upon us and needing us.

And let us, above all things, never forget that in due course the dead will come back, and we never know when we shall see looking out at us from the eyes of a little child a soul we have known. Let us therefore, seeking expression for the love that now has no earthly outlet, turn it to the endeavour to make the world a better place for the return of those we love. This service at least we can do them. That no repining of ours shall make bitter their journey, and that as far as lies in our power the rough places of the world shall be made smooth against their return.

2
Crossing The Threshold

When all that medical science can do has been exhausted, those who stand in the death-chamber awaiting the end are filled with an overwhelming sense of impotence; they have the desire to help, but the total inability to find any adequate practical expression thereof. The consolations of religion may comfort those to whom the spiritual life is a reality, but for many it is no more than a vague hope, and for some, a negation. Have we anything to offer to these?

Yes, we have. We can offer them knowledge. Knowledge derived from the experience of many, many souls who have crossed the great gulf and returned to tell us of their adventures; and also from the experiences of those others, fewer, perhaps, but for us more convincing, who can remember their past lives. In Europe they are rarely to be met with among adults, but many children, before the shades of the prison-house of worldly things close about them, can give us memories of past lives if we ask wisely. In the East such memories are common being the rule rather than the exception.

This knowledge concerning the hidden life of the soul can not only give courage and comfort to the doubting, but can be the means of actively helping those who are passing over. We need no longer stand with empty hands at the bedside of the dying. Though our hands may find nothing more to do, our minds should be active, and we should be making ourselves ready to accompany our friends on the first stage of their journey. We can literally "set them on their way " as we would do with the parting guest.

But before we can consider exactly what may be done for the departing, we must first understand the process of the putting off of the flesh.

There are two kinds of death, natural death and violent death; and there are also two kinds of passing, the peaceful passing, which is normal, and the unpeaceful one, which is pathological. For dying is no less a natural process than being born, and has its norm and its pathologies.

Natural death is that which takes place gradually, the soul loosening itself from the body before its departure just as a child's milk teeth become loose in the socket and fall out painlessly. Violent death, however, is like the pulling of a tooth by the dentist. There is a wrench, a shock, and some bleeding and soreness. Normally, however, the Great Anaesthetist gets in his work rapidly, and with the first opening of the line of cleavage between soul and body, the Greater Sleep descends upon us and we know no more. Where, however, there is much fear of death, or a desperate clinging to life, the work of the Great Anaesthetist is frustrated, and then are seen those terrible death-beds when the soul goes out struggling.

This should never take place, and need never take place where there is adequate knowledge of the processes of death and the after-death life. The dying man should surrender himself into the hands of the Merciful Angel with the same confidence and attitude that he would submit to the offices of the physician who is giving the anaesthetic that is going to shield his consciousness from the work of the surgeon. As soon as the ether gets in its merciful work, the pain and fear will fade and he will sleep for a while knowing nothing. And so it is with death, the Dark Angel closes one by one the avenues of consciousness, and we sleep within ourselves while the processes of the separation of body and soul go on. When all is over, then we are freed from the body, the Angel will re-open the gates of awareness on a higher plane, and we shall live again, though in another dimension. We may find it difficult to realise the kind of life to which we shall open our eyes as the day dawns once more, but we may rest assured that when we awaken on the next life, it will appear to us as normal and natural as the Earth-life to which we are accustomed because we shall find that we are adapted to it.

The soul that goes to meet death with understanding, invoking the merciful offices of the Grey Angel and welcoming his healing ministrations, will draw out from our bourne of Time and Space as quietly as a great ship putting to sea. The changes come gradually, there is no shock or surprise, and as one shore fades, the further one begins to rise above the sky-line.

Insensibly we have drawn away from the body without noticing it. The lower consciousness is now deeply anaesthetised. The higher consciousness is opening, and we find ourselves in what has been called by various names, but which we will call the Body of Light. This is not the same thing as the Etheric Double, or subtle, magnetic, aspect of the physical body. It is this which is anaesthetised by the Grey Angel, for it is in this that the physical processes of death go on; but we know nothing about them, any more than we know of the operation that is performed upon us while we are under chloroform.

It is not everyone, however, who falls into a deep sleep when passing through the Gates of Death. Souls with any degree of psychic development pass out in full consciousness. For although the physical body lapses into insensibility, we should not take it for granted that the soul is unconscious. Anyone who has had experience of trance knows that this is not necessarily so, and that consciousness can be transferred from the body to the soul and retained unimpaired. It is this which happens in death. The consciousness is transferred from the body to the soul and the soul departs to its own place on the Inner Planes, taking the consciousness with it.

It may be wondered whether the soul will not be lonely and forlorn when it first arrives in the Heaven-world, but all who have returned to tell us about the pathway of death, and they are very many, agree that this is not the case. The Heaven-World appears familiar to the newcomer, and for this reason, we are all accustomed to go there in sleep every night!

There is a sleep-life of the soul of which the average person is unaware because he does not bring back the memory upon waking. It is beyond the realm of dream, which is purely subconscious, and the soul of little psychic development remains sound asleep while out of the body, or at best drowsy, and difficult to rouse. It is the rousing of the soul to consciousness upon this plane which produces the dreams which are not like ordinary dreams, of which many people have had experience.

The psychically developed person is at a great advantage when it comes to passing through the Gates of Death, for he goes over in full consciousness. He does not sleep the sleep of death, he merely loses consciousness of the physical plane while retaining all his faculties. Anyone who has ever experienced trance with retained memory, or a lucid dream, has died and risen again, and he will find that death is exactly the same.

But although the Heaven-world will not prove to unfamiliar to us, seeming rather like the home of early childhood revisited, we are nevertheless not left comfortless. There is organised charity in the next world just as there is here, and there are disembodied souls who give themselves to the work of receiving and ministering to the newcomers, companioning them until they feel at home.

It is well known how often dying people exclaim they see a great light, and in that light are the faces of friends and relatives who have passed out before them. Whenever there is a strong bond of love between souls on different sides of the gulf of death, those on the far side invariably come down to the shore to welcome the newcomer upon his arrival.

It is a great thing to know that as the physical world recedes from us, the coast of the next world is rising above the horizon of consciousness, and on that shore will be awaiting our coming all those who have loved us and who have gone before us into the Unseen. We shall land amid familiar faces, as the last words of many a passing soul, calling a greeting, give evidence.

But what of those who have no close ties with any in the next world. Are they left comfortless? No, indeed. They will be met by those who knew unrequited love while on earth, and who have given to the service of all the love which was not needed by the one. There come to meet the friendless ones those who have in their own lives achieved the ideals however dimly realised and rarely glimpsed, which appealed to each soul as the noblest goal of life; and by their help the soul goes forward to its lessons and its achievements.

3
Helping Or Hindering The Dead

The question of communication with the departed has always been a vexed one. On the one hand we have those who deny its possibility and say that all so-called communications are either fraud, delusion, or credulity; on the other are those who admit the possibility of traffic with the dead, but call it necromancy and condemn it unsparingly. Meanwhile, those who have lost dear ones have recourse in rapidly increasing numbers to mediums who act, or claim to act, as psychic telephones between this world and the next.

It is agreed by those who have extended experience in the matter, that although communication with the departed is by no means universally to be condemned, it needs to be approached with caution under carefully chosen conditions, and a state of extreme grief and desperate emotional upheaval is certainly not the ideal condition under which an approach should be made. Sometimes the state of mind of the bereaved is such that it is advisable for the dead to return to give the desired assurance, but to do so is an act of self-sacrifice on their part, and nothing can possibly be worse for the departing soul than to be called back repeatedly to communicate with those left behind. To hold the soul to physical life in this way is an act of great, though, no doubt unintentional selfishness; it disturbs the one who has entered into the light, and prevents him from settling down in his new conditions. It is just as if a fond mother placed her child at a boarding school, and then kept on sending for him and weeping over her loneliness and lamenting the parting. What would be the state of mind of a child who was treated like that? He would get no pleasure from his new companions and his sports, nor profit from his lessons. We, if we keep on calling the departed back to us through the instrumentality of a medium, are acting just as unwisely and selfishly as the foolish mother.

As soon as this life ends, the next life begins, and the dead have their own work to do. We must be content to let them do it freely and in their own way, just as a woman, however loving and beloved, must be content to let her husband or son go forth to do their work in the world.

It is noticeable in the communications received from the departed that the newly dead are fairly accessible to communication, and then, after a while, they seem to go on to a further plane where communication ceases to be possible. If we keep on calling them back, they cannot make this transition and become earthbound. The process of death is incomplete, and they cannot enter into their rest. While therefore it may be justifiable, or even advisable, to reestablish communication with those who have just passed over, it is in every way undesirable to keep up this communication unduly. It should be enough for us that those who have passed out send us word of their safe arrival upon the other shore. Having received that we ought to rest content.

The state into which the dead enter immediately after departure is an intermediate and transitional state, and it is one in which certain definite postmortem pathologies can occur. Cases in which all has not gone well are delayed there, awaiting the working out of their problems. Normally, the soul passes swiftly through this phase and leaves it behind. Delay at this stage is very undesirable. The soul should be speeded on its journey, and it is for this purpose that the Catholic Church says masses for the dead; these masses are of great value, and the principle should be reintroduced into the liturgies of all faiths. We should not think that we have rendered the last office to the dead when the funeral service has been said over them, but the consolations of religion should follow them right through this transition stage until they are well established in their new life. As long as any shreds of earth ties linger, the protection and guidance of organised religion should be available to the soul.

This intermediate stage between life and death is not the same thing as Purgatory. It is rather a landing-stage whereon the soul steps ashore and gathers together its baggage and greets its friends. Purgatory might be defined as a psychic quarantine.

It is only after consciousness has accustomed itself to the disembodied life that the soul goes on to face the purification of Purgatory. Let it be clearly realised that Purgatory is not punitive, nor is it eternal, but consists in forcing the soul to face its own record. It is the reactions of the soul to that record which are the cleansing fires. Purgatory is not a place, but a state of consciousness; but because, on the Inner Planes, all those with the same outlook draw together, Purgatory for all practical psychic purposes has a definite astral location.

It is while souls are going through their purgatory that the threads of communication with this world are severed. Each soul must enter into the silence in order to pass through the cleansing fires. No one can help them there. They must stand upon their own feet and walk by such light as they have. Not otherwise can they learn their lessons. We can no more learn for another than we can eat for another. We must surrender our loved ones into the hands of the Lords of Karma when this point is reached. We have this comfort, however, that it is their aim to make, not to break the soul, and no one is given more than they can bear, nor even more than they can assimilate and turn to good use.

The esotericist would not agree with the Catholic teaching that masses for the dead can help a soul in purgatory. He holds that the value of the prayers of priest and friends is in the influence they have upon the soul during the intermediate period; once the soul has passed through this phase it finds its place in the great cycle of life on the Inner Planes and will be cared for.

After the soul has drawn clear of Purgatory it is not only possible but legitimate to reestablish communication with it, provided the right methods are used. If we are able to raise consciousness to the higher psychic planes, we can of our own volition come into telepathic touch with the departed and hear their voice with the inner ear. It is not advisable to try and see them with the psychic vision, because this belongs to a lower sub-plane of the Astral to that upon which the blessed departed, cleansed from their sins, are privileged to abide. Clairaudience is the right method to use in communication with those who have passed to the heaven-world.

It will be noticeable that descriptions of the heaven-world are nearly always second-hand; the psychic is told what that world is like, but does not actually see it. There are, of course, exceptions to this general rule in the case of exceptionally gifted psychics, or exceptional circumstances, but generally speaking it will be found to hold good, and we may know that if we see the departed with psychic vision, they are still in the intermediate world, and that when they have arrived safely in the heaven-world we shall hear but not see them when they attempt direct communication.

When we are trying to get into touch with them, therefore, we should listen, but not look; and in the still small voice of the inner consciousness we may not unreasonably expect to hear at least a word of greeting; once contact is established, there will be times when we shall get a distinct impression of a presence so tangible that we feel we have only to stretch out the hand to touch it; but if we open our eyes we shall find nothing there.

The dead, upon their plane, are minds without bodies, and when they speak, they speak to our mental, and not, to our bodily senses. That is to say, it is the intuition that perceives them, and not the sight.

It is good that normal, intuitional communication should be established between the dead and the living, for it robs death of its terrors. We ought to look upon the dead as living in another state of consciousness, not another place. If we can "tune in" to their vibration, we can hear them and speak to them. In fact we can speak to them much more readily than we can hear them, for the dead, being bodiless, are normally psychic. It is for this reason that we should guard our thoughts carefully in relation to the dead, and especially strive to overcome our grief and learn to acquiesce in their departure. Our attitude towards the dead should be the same as it would if they had set out to seek their fortunes overseas. We would send to an emigrating son or lover a word of good cheer to hearten him in his distant enterprise. If we continually sent a tale of woe, enlarging on our own sufferings in his absence, could we expect our letters to be eagerly welcomed? Would they not rather be dreaded as an ordeal? What should be our aim? To help and encourage and hearten the dead, or to indulge our own grief and relieve our feelings at their expense? The parting and the loneliness, the loss of the breadwinner and protector, or the lifelong companion, are indeed a grief, but a grief to be bravely borne in order that our darkness may not overshadow the beloved one. We ought to accept our lot cheerfully so that they may be free to go through the great experiences of the soul and enter into their rest with a quiet mind.

4
The Overcoming Of Grief

The way in which we face bereavement is one of the greatest tests of our spiritual understanding. Our attitude towards the death of the body, whether our own or that of one dear to us, depends upon what we really believe life to be. Do we, in our hearts, look upon the physical body as the real man, and all it means to us upon the physical plane as constituting our relationship with the soul we love, incarnated in that body? Then how can we do otherwise than lament our irreparable loss when death breaks the frail vessel that holds our loved one? But do we actually know, from our experience of inner things, that man is a spiritual being, eternal and immortal? Then we shall be able to look beyond the death of the body to the life that is hid with Christ in God.

There is more than one kind of love, and bereavement will reveal which kind is ours. The lowest kind of love is more of a hunger than anything else. We hunger for affection and care and attention. Suddenly thrown upon our own resources by bereavement we feel the pangs of emotional starvation.

Another kind of love, and one that is not so very much higher than the obviously selfish kind, relieves an emotional tension by pouring out demonstrative affection and service upon the beloved one, without stopping to inquire too closely what his needs may be. This kind of love, suddenly denied its outlet and thrown back upon itself, shakes the nature to its foundations and is responsible for many breakdowns after bereavement.

It may seem a strange thing to say, but true love is not emotional in its nature, but is an attitude of the soul towards life. True love is a spiritual radiation, like sunlight, and like the sun, it shines upon the evil and the good, the just and the unjust, not blind to their condition, but loving them just the same. This is the noblest love, and it has healing in its wings.

True love proceeds from a loving nature, not from stimulated emotions. It is the only kind which will make for happiness in marriage or any other relation of life, and it is not this kind of love that leads to mental breakdowns and extremities of grief when the beloved one is removed by death.

It is true there must always be shock and emptiness when one upon whose love we have leant for years is taken from us, for the whole life must be readjusted; but the shock should not be of such a nature as to bring the whole structure of existence crashing down. If it does this, we may know that we have broken the Second Commandment. We have made a graven image and worshiped it, instead of knowing and serving the one true God.

There can be but one true centre of life, and that is God. We may have companions and dear comrades upon the path of life, but life itself has only one centre. If the hub of a wheel is anywhere save in the exact centre, the wheel is out of the true, and useless. We and our loved ones are like spokes in the wheel of life, but for both them and us the hub should be God. When we try to throw the weight of our life upon one spoke, instead of upon the hub, we are making a radical mistake, a mistake that throws us out of balance upon all planes.

If we and those we love are God-centred, death will bring no sense of inner isolation, for we shall know that they have gone on ahead of us to the goal at which we were mutually aiming. If they were to return to us after they have passed over, they would say, as did the Risen Christ to the disciples who were mourning His loss, "Lo, I go before you into Galilee."

To those who are united in spirit, death is but a temporary severance. There must be loneliness, and there must be burdens to be shouldered alone that were once shared by the other, but there is not that sense of spiritual annihilation which devastates those who have laid up their treasure where moth and rust corrupt.

It is this inner certainty of an enduring bond which is the sheet-anchor in times of bereavement. For many, it is a certainty which no materialistic philosophy, no logical demonstration of mortality can affect. They may not understand the grounds upon which their certainty rests. To them it may be a blind belief, admittedly illogical. Nevertheless it is there, a fact of the inner life.

The mystic, however, with this knowledge of the Inner Planes, is able to explain this feeling and show that it is a true psychic intuition, and by no means illogical. On the Inner Planes there is neither time nor space as we understand it. We are near to those with whom we are in emotional rapport, and far from those with whom we are emotionally out of tune. When there is a real tuning of two souls, they are literally together on the Inner Planes, where to be of one mind is to be in one place. Do we not know only too well that it is possible to share bed and board, and yet be as apart as the stars? Equally is it a fact of inner experience that if there is a true spiritual union, we remain in touch, wherever our bodies may be.

If we observe life, we shall see how true this is. There is a subtle difference between a man or a woman who is well and truly mated and one who is not. They need not to be together for this to be apparent, for it is a subtle psychological difference, and separation does not affect it. The man or woman who loves and is loved retains that sense of spiritual fulfilment even when separated for long periods. It is well known to psychologists that the lack of this mating, which is called by esotericists Polarisation, is responsible for many nervous illnesses, and that these can occur even in marriage if there is no spiritual affinity and companionship.

If we continue to love and be loved, even after the loss of the loved one, this spiritual widowing does not occur, and we are not left unmated. The intangible influence of the love continues to make itself felt, and the personality remains polarised.

The bond of physical union weakens with the passing of youth. The bond of emotional union is broken with the withdrawal of the personality from physical sight, but the bond of spiritual union survives all severance whether of space or time and continues to inspire and to protect both of those who are held in its tie, upon whatever plane they may be.

The bond of spiritual union reveals itself in a common idealism, a comradeship in the things of the spirit. Where this exists, it will endure as long as the spirit endureth, for it is as eternal as God who gave it. This spiritual communion continues uninterruptedly through the death of the body and all the after death experiences of the soul. It needs no psychic powers to bring it within reach of mundane consciousness. It is like the sound of a brook; we may not hear it when we are busy with the toil of affairs, but in the quiet of the night, when all sounds are stilled, we hear the purl of the running water, going steadily on, hour after hour, and we know that it has been sounding all day, although we have not heard it.

When spiritual love is coming to us from the Inner Planes we have only to still the outer senses for a moment to hear it purling like the brook, a steady flow, coming to us all the time from the eternal and steadfast soul that has gone on ahead to the Next Country. And we on our side, if we still love, may send out an equally steady flow to comfort our beloved. Let us therefore gather up all our courage so that the brook of love may not carry the debris of dead hopes on to the Inner Planes, to be perceived psychically by our loved one to his distress. Let us keep our hopes alive by working for the ideals that were dear to us both. So can we make a channel through which those ideals may still come to fruition, for our comradeship with our beloved can continue in the Path of Service.

5
The Appointed Time

We do not wish to have towards death the fatalistic attitude of the Muslim, however much we may admire his courage; nor yet the panic-stricken clinging to life of many so-called Christians. Whoever has any knowledge of astrology knows that the time when death is likely to occur can be predicted with considerable accuracy; but if he has had any practical experience of the same art, he also knows that that which is threatened does not necessarily befall. There are a great many factors to be taken into consideration in a horoscope, and the judgment is after all not the answer to a sum in arithmetic, concerning which there can be only one result, but the opinion of the astrologer concerning the ultimate outcome of an indefinite number of counterbalancing factors. Astrology is much more of an art than a science, and the personal factor in both querent and astrologer is a very large one.

No one can deny, however, that there are tides of death in every horoscope, tides on which the soul may readily slip across the harbour-bar into the Great Beyond. The cords are loosened then, and if a sudden stress comes, they may part. On the other hand, a compensating force may come into play; the faith or the will-power of the querent himself, or of one close to him, may suffice to hold the soul in the body till the tide has run its course and the knot of life tightens again automatically. In such a case we may literally say that a new lease of life has been entered upon, and that there is little likelihood of death until the planets once again have moved into a fatal position. It is very instructive to retrogress a horoscope, if such a term may be permitted, and observe how the planets stood during periods of crisis in the past. We shall find that there may have been more than one period when the Angel of Death drew near but passed by. What has happened once may happen again, and it is as unwise to assume the certainty of death before the breath is out of the body as it is to count chickens before they are hatched.

One thing is certain—if life be trembling in the balance, the knowledge that an astrologer has passed sentence of death will be a very powerful depressant and may serve to turn the balance. In my opinion, however clearly death may appear to be written in a horoscope, no astrologer should ever reveal the fact, but should content himself with saying that the period will be a critical one for the health of the querent. This will be sufficient to give warning without inducing a paralysing auto-suggestion.

We may assume, then, that there are periods when the soul is liable to go out, but is not necessarily bound to go out. These periods must necessarily be times of anxiety, but we need not adopt a fatalistic attitude towards them and lie down and die without a struggle because our planets are adverse. Mars may have something to say to Saturn, and may say it effectually.

It cannot be other than a misfortune if death comes before the age of three score years and ten, because in each incarnation a long period of preparation has to be undergone before maturity of the faculties is reached and we begin to reap what we have sown. To have to undergo another period of infancy, childhood, and youth before full return has been obtained from the investment of life-values has been obtained in the present period is a misfortune, though not necessarily a tragedy if seen against the wide landscape of evolving life. We should reinforce by every means in our power the battle against a premature death; but after our allotted span, unless we have work to finish, we are wise to take our quittance when it comes, going tranquilly out with the tide, secure that our life is hid with Christ in God. It is better to go and take a new body than cling to one that is fast becoming uninhabitable. If we have passed the allotted span, we may well say, "Lord, now suffer Thou Thy servant to depart in peace."

By this I do not mean it to be understood that we should refuse ordinary precautions and remedial measures. It is our duty to fulfil the laws of Nature as long as we are under the jurisdiction of those laws. It is the attitude of mind to which I refer. We may fight death grimly to the last ditch, holding body and soul together with all the power of a concentrated will; or we may turn our thoughts to the heaven-world and begin to reach out towards it. Before three score years and ten it is our duty to fight death with spiritual resources as well as material; but after that time, unless there is some definite reason to the contrary, such as obligations unfulfilled, or work unfinished, we do best to place ourselves in God's hands, for He will not recall His servant until his work is done and the time of rest is due.

We must never forget that spiritual law and karma are not the same thing. It is karma that causes the premature death of the body, but it is spiritual law that withdraws the soul from incarnation when the time is ripe. Spiritual forces can be used to counteract an evil karma, but there is nothing that either could or should be used to counteract spiritual law. Our greatest good lies in fulfiling it.

We must get out of the way of thinking that death is the ultimate tragedy. There are conditions under which it may be a misfortune for all concerned, both for the passing soul and those around him. But on the other hand, it may be the next stage in life! It is only the man sunk in matter who calls the Angel of Death the Great Enemy. His esoteric name is the Opener of the Gates of Life.

6

Traditional Custom and Psychic Fact

There are many old customs connected with the passing of a soul which have their roots in psychic fact and are not merely superstitions. Some, of course, are pre-Christian in origin and their usefulness has passed away; others are still valid, and it is helpful to observe them.

Among these is the beautiful custom of placing candles and fresh flowers in the death-chamber as soon as the soul has departed. There is a brief interregnum between the disanimation of the physical body and the withdrawal of the soul from the etheric double. During this period the soul remains close to its physical vehicle, gradually disentangling itself from the meshes of matter and reorientating itself to its new state. The etheric double, cut off from the supply of prana, or etheric vitality, which it derives from the sun while in incarnation, and not yet adjusted to its new condition, is apt to draw this vitality from whatever source may be available to it. This fact accounts for the sudden feeling of exhaustion and depletion, or even fear, which not infrequently comes to those whose duties cause them to be in the immediate neighbourhood of dead bodies unless they have shielded themselves behind the armour of callousness. Those who have loved the dead are especially susceptible to this form of depletion.

Now it is undoubtedly a humane act to companion departed souls with thoughts of love and protection while they are going through the period of adjustment; and we may even, in certain cases, feel it wise to permit a soul that has gone out in fear and distress to cling for a while to our physical vitality before persuading it to take up the task of living its new life. These things have to be wisely and compassionately judged. We should always bear in mind, however, that the help we give to the dead should be directed towards helping them to make the transition to their new life, and not towards maintaining them in an intermediate state, which may lead to their acquiring the habit of death-in-life, and so becoming earth-bound.

There is a great difference between a mental rapport and an etheric rapport. The latter is not a desirable thing; it rapidly becomes pathological for both the living and the dead and should never be suffered to establish itself.

There will, however, always be an instinctive, involuntary reaching out after etheric vitality by the etheric double pending the commencement of its disintegration, and we can not only protect the living, but help the dead by understanding the nature of this phenomenon and acting accordingly.

Fire is an elemental form of etheric life, and the unguarded flame of a candle, fully exposed to the air, emanates a not inconsiderable proportion of etheric substance. If we place lighted candles round the death-bed and cover it with fresh flowers, there will be available sufficient etheric emanations to meet the needs of the etheric double, tide it over its transition stage, and prevent it from drawing upon the vitality of the living. This is in every way more natural than allowing the dead to get into what may well end by being an unwholesome rapport with those who are left behind, and is at the same time more humane than affording them no help at all.

It is not right to leave the dead alone and neglected in the interval between their passing and the funeral of the body, when the final quittance is given; neither is it desirable or necessary to maintain a continual watch beside them; but three times each day, at morning, noon, and night, it is well to kneel in prayer beside the body, or, if this be not possible, to project the thoughts towards the spot where it lies, and imagine ourselves to be kneeling there as we pray. This is a great help to the departed, and should never be neglected, for, next to Christian burial, it is the greatest service we can render the dead.

It is not a good thing to burn incense in the death-chamber, because the fumes of incense lend themselves too easily to a materialisation, and it is our aim to help the departing soul to pass as swiftly and easily as may be through the phases of death and enter into the spiritual life, so that it may not linger within the atmosphere of earth wherein the pathologies of death occur.

The drawing of the blinds when a death takes place is another custom which has its roots in psychic fact. Nothing disperses an etheric double so quickly as sunlight, and it is in order that the processes that follow immediately upon the withdrawal of the soul from the body may not be unduly hastened that the blinds are drawn, the sunlight shut out, and the living flames of candles alone used to light the death-chamber.

An exception should be made to this rule, however, when the nature of the disease has been such that partial death of the tissues has taken place before the death of the body as a whole, or when processes of disintegration follow rapidly upon the passing of the soul, as is the case with certain diseases. For this means that the etheric double has been almost out of the body before the actual end; there is therefore no need to await its disentangling, and the sooner the etheric substance returns to the soul of nature, the better.

The wearing of deep mourning has a very marked psychic effect. Black insulates the wearer from etheric vibrations, and a person so clad is more readily able to get in touch with the subtler planes than one clad in colours, which each attract their corresponding vibration.

The custom of tolling the church bell, however, is as pagan as the keening and wailing at an Irish wake. It is intended to drive away evil spirits and need have no place in Christian burial.

It is a great mistake, nay, a blasphemy, to think of our loved ones as dead, or to associate them with the dust that is returning to the earth whence it came. We should think of the vital mind, the ever-living and aspiring spirit, going up and on with its evolution and calling us to comradeship in that great adventure. It is for this reason that, from the esoteric standpoint, cremation is so much better than burial, for it frees not only the soul of the dead, but the soul of the living. We cannot cling to a handful of dust flying in the wind as we can to a body committed to the ground, returning slowly to Mother Earth.

The last earthly service of love should be to take the ashes of the beloved one to some spot sacred to the memory of happiness, and there scatter them on the wind, giving back to Nature that which Nature gave. There, as at an altar dedicated to love's memory, may we seek to re-establish our contact, not with the dead, but with the Everliving, sending forth our thoughts like birds into the Unseen. It is seldom that they will return to us without the green leaf of hope.

But we cannot do this as long as we identify in thought our loved one with the dead body. Let us return that body to the elements at the earliest possible moment in order that we may free our love from the sense of death. Where cremation is not possible, then I would plant upon the grave some strong-growing tree or shrub that shall draw up the etheric life from the earth and give it to the air. I have seen graves that are little gardens; not sealed with a stone, but full of life and beauty. Between the making of the grave and the placing of the stone there must elapse a period of at least a year, and what can be more beautiful than to sow wheat upon the bare earth to symbolise the life that is given of God? For there is a legend that wheat does not belong to the evolution of our earth, but was brought from another planet by that Great One who came without father, without mother, without descent, having neither beginning of days nor end of life.

Somewhere in the decoration of gravestone or coffin it is invariable to find the Cross. Unfortunately, in our ignorance of the science of symbolism, it is almost invariably the Calvary Cross that is represented. There are many different forms of the Cross, however, and the Calvary Cross represents sacrifice, and renunciation; it is the Keltic Cross, with its long, tapering upright, and small arms, upon which is superimposed a circle, which is the sign of Life Triumphant unto Salvation. This is the Cross beneath which all that is mortal of an initiate should take its rest.

To enclose a body in a leaden shell is a relic of barbarism. The soul has finished with the body and cast it off. Why should we seek to preserve it? The best casket for the mortal remains of those we love is one that will restore them to the earth as speedily as may be. For this reason the traditional elm is better than oak, which is too enduring. If it is not possible to commit the clay to the swift and purifying fire, let the kindly earth perform its office in its own way, returning the elements of mortality each to its place in nature. The soul is not really free until this has been done. Some shadow of earth will remain to cloud its awakening.

7
The Death of the Body

The human body is a machine, dependent for integrity of its parts and the supply of its working, like any other machine, upon the fuel. It is a machine for generating energy, the energy which is employed by the personality in the process of spiritual unfoldment; for it is by means of the experiences undergone when in the body that the soul gathers together the raw material which it works upon in the process of evolution. The occultist is therefore not sentimental over the physical body but endeavours to keep it in good repair while he has it, because good work cannot be done with a bad tool.

We should learn to think of death as part of the processes of growth. A caterpillar dies as a worm to be reborn as a butterfly. In many of the lower forms of existence the cycle of life goes on under our eyes. In the higher forms, however, part of the cycle takes place in the visible sphere of matter and part of it in the invisible sphere of mind. What we call birth is the process of taking on a physical body, and what we call death is a process of discarding it; and as the processes of birth include more than the labour, so do the processes of death include more than the passing of the breath.

If, of course, by death we simply mean the stopping of the human machine, then death is an instantaneous occurrence, such as it is popularly believed to be. But if by death we mean the sum total of the processes which constitute the transition from one phase of existence to another, we are speaking of death as the esotericist understands it, and it is in this sense that we shall consider it in these pages.

There are two ways in which death may come: naturally, and in accordance with divine law; or unnaturally, as a breach of divine law. Strange as it may seem, the esotericist does not reckon death by disease as among the natural deaths. Disease is due to a breach of God's law; in some way violence has been done to Nature, and the breakdown of the human machine is the result.

Natural death, the death brought about by the workings of divine law, only takes place when the karma allotted for that incarnation has been worked out. Until this is done, the vital forces will keep old age at bay and retain the powers but little abated to an advanced age, as is proved by the many instances of men and women strong in God's service far beyond the allotted span of three score years and ten.

Natural death only takes place owing to the wearing out of the working parts of the machine, or, to change the metaphor to a more exact one, to the silting up of the tissues. The machine depends for its working upon the balance of intake and output technically known as metabolism. The intake is always in excess of the normal output in order that there may be a reserve available for emergencies. In childhood and adolescence this extra intake is absorbed in growth; during maturity in reproduction. That which is not absorbed in physical reproduction is, or should be, worked off in some emotionally satisfying pursuit, whether of work or play. As soon as the upbuilding phase of life is past, the surplus of intake or output begins to be stored in the tissues in its most compact chemical forms. Hence the wise and witty saying that a man is as old as his arteries.

There are various ways in which natural death may come. As time goes on, the heart finds it more and more difficult to pump the blood through the increasingly inelastic channels of the arteries; the blood supply to the various organs becomes inadequate, and one or another may in consequence get out of order and cease to function, thus depriving the system of some essential product or service, and so stopping the machine. Or one of the smaller arteries, usually in the brain, may become so weakened that it can no longer cope with the increasing pressure of the blood pumped by a still adequate heart, and finally bursts, causing the well known phenomenon of a "stroke." Equally, the heart on its part may no longer be able to overcome the resistance of the arteries, and finally stops its rhythmical drive at the time of lowest vitality, usually the small hours of the night, and the person "dies in his sleep." This is the true, normal, harmonious form of death. It is ushered in, not by any definite disease, but by a gradually increasing tendency to fatigue, revealed (and compensated) by the steady rising of the tide of sleep, more and more of the twenty-four hours being spent in tranquil oblivion, until finally consciousness is withdrawn and never returns. It is thus that the soul passes when it has fulfiled its tasks and has no more to do in the earth-life of that incarnation.

The unnatural, or pathological death of the body is brought about by some external agency; either the mechanical injury of a vital part; the poisoning of the vital processes, whether by some substance taken into the body, or by the excrete of bacteria that have found lodgment in the tissues; or by the deprivation of an adequate supply of some factor necessary to the fuelling of the machine, whether it be food, vitamins, water, air or sunlight.

Every ill that flesh is heir to will find a place in one of these three categories, and the esotericist regards them all as forms of pathological death, for, given different conditions, they could all have been avoided. If the injury had not taken place, the man would have lived. If he had not come into contact with the virulent germ, the trouble would not have started. If he had had adequate supplies of the necessities of life, neither too much, so that the issues were replete, or too little, so that they were enfeebled, he would have been alive today. We can always say of these pathological forms of death that if such and such a thing had not happened, the dead would not have died. Therefore we say that these deaths are all unnatural, and if we were living in the golden age of the earth's perfection, they would not have occurred. The normal way of dying is to die in the sleep in extreme old age.

8
Going To Meet Death

I f we are filled with terror at the thought of Death coming for us, let us go to meet him, at our leisure.

This may seem a strange idea, but there is a great deal in it that is essentially sensible and practical. There are several religions, notably the Roman Catholic and the Buddhist, which instruct their followers to meditate regularly upon their own deaths. This is a very valuable discipline, and we should all be the better for pursuing it.

This meditation upon our own deaths, however, should not concern itself with the dissolution of the body. The body is not the real *I*. When it is cast off it is but common clay and we are no longer in any way concerned with it. Let the living care for it for sanitary reasons, not superstitious ones. We should think of ourselves as escaping from the body, getting free from its limitations and begin to imagine the kind of life we shall lead when this occurs. We can see ourselves meeting with those of our friends who have preceded us through the Gates of Death. If death appears to be imminent we may send out telepathic messages to them, asking them to meet us. If we are indeed nearing the Threshold it is not unlikely that some response from them will reach us. We can be quite sure that they will do their best to signal to us across the gulf and tell us to be of good cheer; but unless we have some psychic development we may fail to perceive their answering signals. I may instance a case I once came across where a woman who had recently lost a dearly loved sister was sitting in the firelight one evening trying to get into touch with her telepathically. She tried for same time without success, when her attempts at concentration were disturbed by her sister's dog who was lying at her feet, and who appeared to be hunting in his dreams, as dogs do. Suddenly he woke up and looked about him in surprise as if expecting to see someone, and then rushed from room to room of the house barking joyously. This was the first time he had shown any interest or animation since his mistress's death. My friend was of the opinion that she had succeeded in summoning her sister, but had not been able to perceive her; dogs, however, are notoriously psychic, and the dead woman's pet had sensed her presence, his experience being interpreted in his dream even as our own are, and he awoke so firmly convinced that he had seen his mistress that he ran through every room barking and looking for her. My friend told me that nothing could have been more convincing to her than this simple little manifestation of a dog's experience.

But in addition to those personal friends in whose affection we have confidence, there are others upon the Inner Planes whose companionship we may seek and whose acquaintance we may make even before we pass over. We may recall our Lord's promise "I will not leave you comfortless," and pray to Him that our guide may be made known to us in life, so that we may pass out in confidence when our call comes. There is, however, no purpose in doing this unless death is near, because guides change their tasks on the Inner Planes, the work of meeting the dead being one of the first they are employed upon when they come over, and in due course they pass on to other duties. They only come down to the shore to await our coming when the barque of the soul has cast off its mooring-ropes.

The research that has been done by spiritualists has revealed what very important work goes on in that part of the spirit world which is contiguous to the earth plane. There is abundant evidence from innumerable sources that the bands of invisible helpers are highly organised, and that no soul is allowed to pass out alone and unaided. When a ship is about to sail, she hoists the Blue Peter, and every one who has business with her hastens aboard. When the soul is about to depart from the body, it too flies a signal, and there are those on the Inner Planes whose business it is to watch for those signals and see to it that all travelling souls are guided and guarded and welcomed as they move from out our bourne of Time and Space.

Even when the Star of Death is below the horizon we do well to familiarise ourselves with the nature of the after-life states in order that we may become accustomed to the idea of them and that they may not seem strange or terrible to us. We can rob death of its terrors in this way more effectually than in any other.

Moreover, we may meet someone who is hag ridden by that cruel and terrible fear of death which secretly afflicts so many who have been brought up in the old concepts of death and hell. It is a thing that very few people will confess spontaneously, and to meet someone who has escaped from that bondage may be like a light dawning in darkness to them.

In our meditations upon our own deaths do not let us concentrate so much upon the passing out as upon the life we are entering upon. Let us think joyously of the new hopes and activities that are opening up before us. We shall be free of the cumbrance of the body which, as our time draws near, becomes increasingly a drag upon our activities; we shall rise up in the Body of Light, as it is called by the ancients; the burden of old age and ill health will have fallen from us, and we shall be vigorous of form and clear and buoyant in consciousness. In death we literally take on a new lease of life. We shall enter upon that new life with all the vigour and enthusiasm of youth, for we are indeed born again.

9
The Hidden Side of Death

The processes even of physical death are not nearly so simple as popular imagination believes, and it was a knowledge of the subtler aspects of death that gave rise to many of the funeral practices of the ancients which we look upon today as pure superstition.

With the passing of the breath the soul itself is gone and is no more concerned with its cast-off body than the chick with the egg-shell. But those who remain are concerned with it, and certain of the subtler problems of the shock of bereavement are due to the little-understood processes that are going on the discarded clay.

We have two tasks to perform before our service to our loved one is finished; we must see to it that dust returns to dust as swiftly and harmoniously as possible, giving rise to none of those happenings which may be termed the pathologies of death; and we ought to follow up the departing soul with the right kind of telepathic communication until it is safely established on the Other Side and will want to enter into its rest for a period. These two aspects of the last services to the departed are of very great importance, and we ought to give them our serious attention. Moreover, there is nothing that will help us in our grief so much as to feel that there is still something to be done for those who have gone over, and that we are not free to let ourselves go unreservedly in a paroxysm of emotion as we might do if we felt that we had nothing but ourselves to consider.

Let us study first what happens to the discarded and empty body immediately after the departure of the soul, for this will guide us in our attitude toward it and our manner of dealing with it. Firstly, the departure of the soul only means the death of the central nervous system, there is a great deal of organic life still left in the body itself. It does not die all in one piece. Indeed, for some days before death, or even longer, the soul may have been out of the body, floating at the end of the silver cord a few feet above the bed, looking like a sleeping ghost and clearly visible to any psychic. While this condition prevails there is deep unconsciousness on all planes and no suffering. It is only when the silver cord is severed that the soul finally departs and actual death occurs. The sudden rally and return of consciousness at the end is caused by the soul, which recovers consciousness on its own plane as the end approaches, making a last effort to concentrate on the body in order that the process known to occultists as the etching of the seed-atom may take place effectually.

This seed-atom is a nucleus of force of the same type as that of the physical plane, which is retained by the soul throughout its evolution, and which plays an important part in the processes of rebirth. The term etching is, of course, metaphorical, and represents the tuning of this nucleus to a certain type of vibration and its impression with certain images. If this has already been done, the soul is ripe for death, and the last rally may not take place; therefore the absence of this rally does not mean that the processes of death are not going on as they should. On the other hand, when violent death takes place, if the body is so shattered that death is instantaneous, no etching of the seed-atom is possible. Therefore it is held by esotericists that the soul immediately seeks rebirth, before the second death takes place, and equally rapidly passes out again, having merely assumed a physical body long enough to enable it to make its exit from life in due form. It has often been remarked by mothers and midwives that the new-born child which has an extraordinary appearance of intelligence and maturity in its eyes is not going to live. It is the eyes of an adult soul that they see looking at them, and all the service that soul requires at their hands is the rites of burial according to its faith. It is not meant to live, it is only meant to die adequately.

It may seem that this inflicts a hardship on the mother who has made her great sacrifice to bring it into the world only to lose it; but if we examine the karmic record of the case, and no occultist would ever attempt to judge a matter in the light of a single incarnation, we shall find either that there is a karmic debt owing, which is settled in this way, or if no such debt can be traced, then karmic credit has been given. This karmic credit is a point that is often forgotten. Sometimes the Lords of Karma owe us a debt which entitles us to one of those sudden strokes of pure luck which we can explain by means of no hypothesis which only takes account of one life. The Good Samaritan, the complete stranger who renders us a totally unexpected service, may be a soul for whom we have opened the gates of birth and death in a previous life.

Once the soul has safely withdrawn, however, there is an immediate change. Any sensitive person can feel the difference between the atmosphere of the chamber of death, however peaceful, and the atmosphere of the chamber of the dead. During life, a man is under the lordship of the Archangel of his race and the Saviour of his religion; but after death this domination is withdrawn; or rather, it follows the soul and leaves the body to its own devices as being no longer of any concern. The vacant clay then passes under the domination of the Regents of the Elements, and the elemental forces of earth, air, fire and water each withdraw that which belongs to them and restore it to its own kingdom. In this process they are assisted by a certain type of life which belongs to the most primitive form of existence and which is fast passing out of manifestation, I refer to the unicellular organisms that live on dead matter, the saprophytic bacteria which cause decomposition. The parasitic bacteria which feed upon living tissues and cause disease are another matter. They belong to certain forms of life whose day is overpast and who, defying the law of evolution, refuse to withdraw from the physical plane. They are rebels against cosmic law, and advancing knowledge is gradually driving them out of manifestation.

The curious "feel" of the death-chamber and the fear that most people have of a dead body are caused by this opening of the gates of the elemental kingdoms. The beings of the elements are present and active when organic matter has to be disintegrated and returned to its respective spheres. Sensitive people feel their presence, and because elementals belong to a very primitive form of life, find them disturbing. It is for this reason that it is not good for the living to remain in the immediate neighbourhood of the dead.

There are, however, four mighty Archangels who are called the Archangels of the Elements because they rule the elemental kingdoms as overlords in the name of God. These are Raphael, Michael, Gabriel and Uriel, and they equate with the four Evangelists of the Christian tradition. Hence the child's prayer:

> "Four angels round my bed,
> Two at the foot and two at the head.
> Matthew, Mark, Luke and John,
> Guard the bed that I lie on."

Every rite for the dead ought to commit the clay into the care of these four great spirits before the Throne. When they are invoked it will be found that the somewhat sinister atmosphere sometimes felt in a death-chamber will immediately lift and clear.

The return to dust of the body, however, is but half the process of physical death, for there is another body, equally physical, equally mortal, which is called the etheric double. It might aptly, be called the body of electricity, for it is an organised system of electromagnetic stresses, and in its meshes every cell and fibre of the physical body lies like a bottle in a bottle-rack. It transmits to every molecule of the body the vital force which keeps disintegration at bay and maintains the unstable compounds of organic matter in their elaborate and fugitive forms.

It is the withdrawal of this etheric double which marks the critical moment of death when the breath is seen to pass. Embodied in it the soul remains in an unconscious condition for a brief period, from a few hours to three days; if its tenancy of the etheric body is prolonged beyond this time, or if the soul wakes up to consciousness while still in the etheric double, one of the pathologies of death has occurred.

It is this waking of the soul while still in its etheric double which, in popular phrase, causes its ghost to walk. Within the appointed time, however, unless something abnormal occurs, the magnetic forces of this body of electricity will have been exhausted; it will be like a battery that has run down, and the soul will slip out of its meshes and no longer have any link with matter.

It is not this, however, that we call the Second Death; it is rather the second half of the physical death, and while it is going on the soul is asleep in the deepest unconsciousness. It will now be seen why it is so unwise to try and get into touch with a soul immediately it has passed over, for we may wake it from its etheric sleep and cause it to "walk." Do not let it be thought by this that the esotericist condemns communication with the departed; but there is a right and a wrong way of effecting this communication, and there are times when it may safely and helpfully be done, and times when it had better be left alone, and we need to know these things if we are to deal with death rightly. Our modern thought places adults in the same position in relation to the mysteries of death that children endure in relation to the mysteries of birth; there is a conspiracy of silence which confuses the issue and places us at a grave disadvantage in dealing with our problems.

10
Purgatory

We have already told of the merciful work of the Great Anaesthetist, who causes a deep sleep to fall upon the soul as it passes out of the gates of the flesh. The etheric body fades and falls away from it unnoticed, and it sleeps on in that state of consciousness which occultists call the astral plane.

But presently it begins to dream. The memories of its earth life are still present with it, though faint and far away, like the memories of early childhood. But it does not dream of these happenings as they appear to us who shared them; it reviews them instead from the point of view of its present state of existence. It is in the World of Desire, and it sees them from the standpoint of fulfiled or frustrated desires.

But the brain no longer clogging consciousness, the soul is not only conscious upon the plane of its present existence, but the higher consciousness is also awake and active, and all the time that this phantasmagoria of dream is going on, the higher self is holding up the mirror to consciousness and bidding the soul look therein upon its own image. All the time the inexorable spiritual standards are kept before its eyes. The soul, forced to contemplate these, undergoes a struggle severe in proportion to its deviation from the spiritual standards. Nothing explains these states so well as the terminology of analytical psychology. The soul is in the throes of a conflict between its higher and lower aspects. This conflict is subjective and expresses itself in the imagery of the astral dream, and the soul is said to be in purgatory. For purgatory is simply the forced realisation of the significance of our own misdeeds. Its scenery, so often described by saints and psychics is such stuff as dreams are made on, the dreams of souls forced to face the truth. This scenery, therefore, is by no means idly fantastic, but has definite symbolic relationship to the problems of the soul, of evolution, and of the cosmic reactions. Every soul has its own personal symbolism, derived from the experiences of its own history, even as we find in the psycho-analysis of dreams. In addition to this it has the symbolism of the types of its religious faith, which it shares with all the members of its faith. Therefore the hell of the Christian will differ in many ways from the hell of the Moslem. On the other hand, it will have much in common, because there are certain type-symbols which are common to all sentient human beings, being formed out of their common human experience, such as the pain of burning and the torture of thirst.

Each individual soul is taught by these dream pictures that sin brings inevitable suffering, for it is shown the consequences of its wickedness or folly and may not turn away its eyes. It feels in imagination as it would feel if it had actually come to the state which its dreams depict. Sisyphus the ambitious rolls his eternal stone up the hill and may not rest; Tantalus the drunkard sees the cup recede from his lips. Thus each learns the vanity of his weakness.

The initiate has never believed in the appaling doctrine of eternal punishment. No psychic has ever confirmed this belief, no spirit returned from beyond the grave has ever reported it. What is there any man could do in the brief spell between birth and death to deserve it?

But every spirit reports purgatory and has a wholesome respect for it. But these are not the flames of eternal torment but the cleansing fires that purify the soul as gold is tried in the furnace until all its dross is burned away and it is pure and precious. It is not maintained, however, that the dross of an evolution can all be burnt away in the purgation of a single death. Few souls are so pure and strong that they could endure so severe a trial without their fibres being disintegrated. Therefore we are shown no more at a single purgation than we can well bear and profit by. We are permitted to wipe out a certain proportion of our karma, and then come back to earth with the rest still bound about our neck, and it is this unexpiated karma that causes our suffering in the next life. And so gradually, with what we realise while in purgatory and with what we make amends for while on earth, we compensate our karma and adjust the balance. Thus does the soul make its growth.

But although purgatory is primarily a subjective experience, it is not wholly subjective. The vivid dreams and feelings of the souls going through this experience create a very definite atmosphere about them. On the astral plane there is no time and space as we understand them, but a mood is a place, and those who are in the same emotional state are drawn together. Can we not readily understand how the atmosphere made by all the souls at present out of incarnation who are struggling with thwarted hate or unsatiated lust, would mould the scenery of Hell out of the plastic astral ethers?

All those who hate, all those who lust, congregate together, and it is largely the cumulative atmosphere that they make between them which causes the abreaction of the higher type of soul, the soul that has possibilities of redemption. The minor transgression, which appears venial enough in ourselves, looks very different when we find ourselves in the midst of a sphere where innumerable souls are carrying it to all extremes and we have to live in its atmosphere. Indulgence in the sins of the flesh, which may not appear so bad when it is being done by a single person in an otherwise clean environment, will soon nauseate even its most hardened habitué when he is compelled to practice his chosen vice in company with thousands of others who are all doing exactly the same thing, and is not allowed to stop when he has had enough, because the irresistible momentum carries him on willy-nilly. This is the most effectual way to cure the sins of the flesh, and the Lords of Karma make full use of it.

If, however, a soul has largely risen above its weaknesses during life, or if it is not very deeply imbued with them, its visit to the purgatorial fiery whirlpool will be brief, for its struggle to resist the current will soon cause it to be thrown out upon the bank, free. None, however, may escape the experience of facing their own weaknesses in the company of those like-minded to themselves. No amount of masses and candles and prayers can spare them this. We can, however, concentrate upon souls a telepathic current which shall focus spiritual forces upon them and thus cause them to win to a realisation and reaction more quickly. In brief, we can apply spiritual healing to the souls in purgatory.

Many people endure great anxiety concerning the fate of some loved one who has died in sin and unrepentant. It may be a great comfort to them to know that spiritual healing forces can be applied just as effectually to souls in purgatory as "absent treatment" can be given to souls in incarnation. Let us always remember that if we can communicate telepathically during life, we shall have no difficulty in communicating telepathically after death. For if minds can communicate without material means while both are upon earth, the position will not be materially affected when one of the pair has no longer got any material means wherewith to communicate but has to rely exclusively upon the mind.

One of the occult disciplines consists in reviewing each night the events of the day in the reverse order, that is to say, from the evening to the morning. Although this may be a little confusing at first, for the mind naturally attempts to follow its habitual sequence of cause and effect, one soon becomes habituated to it and experiences no difficulty. There is a twofold reason for this operation. The first is to accustom the mind to work out of its normal sequence and so enable it to penetrate the veil of birth and recover memories of past incarnations, and the other is to keep the karmic debt within bounds. By abreacting each day any errors we may have made, we prevent our purgatorial debt from accumulating. Of course, if we merely abreact them each day and repeat them again the next, we are not doing ourselves very much good, for although we may have neutralised that particular portion of karma, we are acquiring plenty more of an even more unpleasant nature, for we are making sure of a place for ourselves in the hell reserved for hypocrites, and anything more painful than the unmasking of a hypocrite to the depths of his selfish and cowardly soul it is hard to imagine. The mills of God grind exceeding small and not so slowly either, all things considered.

Let us always bear in mind, however, that purgatory is neither punitive nor retributive, but essentially healing to the soul. The cautery of fire clears up the septic wounds that life has left us. There is clean healing after that burning. Let us therefore, during our lifetime, clear up all we can of those things we have done amiss, whether in wickedness, error, or weakness. If we can cure ourselves of our evil tendencies purgatory will not have to teach us our lessons, for we shall have already learnt them. And finally, when our time comes to die, let us go over with courage, knowing that our evil dream will not last long; going to our purgatory as we would go to the dentist, knowing that it is going to be more or less painful, but not more than flesh and blood can bear and be none the worse for it. And let us, above all, realise that we are in skilled hands.

11
The Heaven–World

We hear a great deal about the Heaven-world in Spiritualistic communications, and many people are repulsed by the idea, for they feel that everything is represented as being so material. They read of Raymond smoking cigars and drinking champagne and feel that Heaven falls short of their expectations. Or again they read of a golden floor and perpetual harping, and feel that this would not appeal to them either. A rather higher type of Heaven is described by the spirits, who tell us that the artist paints marvellous pictures upon illimitable canvas; or the scientist penetrates the secrets of nature by merely looking at them. Delightful as everything is made to sound, we feel instinctively that there is something wrong, for all this does not ring true. Moreover, we feel that we should be thoroughly bored even if it were true, for there is no pleasure in an age-long, effortless perfection. So much of our joy in achievement lies in the triumph of difficulties overcome. There can be no such joy in an effortless Heaven.

For many people, too, there could be no joy in a Heaven that did not include their loved ones.

Now what are we to say to all these contradictory statements which do violence to our deepest instincts? They cannot all be right. But nevertheless, are they all wrong? How are we to understand them? First of all we must realise that Heaven is a state of consciousness, not a place. Pure mind is independent of time and space, as we know by our dreams, whether the dream of sleep or the day dream. We can phantasy ourselves to be in ancient Egypt or far Cathay, and for all the purposes of consciousness we are there for the moment. We see the sights, we hear the sounds of these times and places in proportion to the vividness of our imagination.

When we are first dead, we are simply disembodied minds and obey the laws of dream consciousness. Purgatory is our dream of remorse and purification, and the Heaven-world is our wish-fulfilment. Freud tells the story of the little boy whose ration of cherries was limited by a careful mother, and who on awakening next morning announced, "Hermann has eaten all the cherries." His dream had fulfiled the ungratified wish of the previous day.

So in the sleep of death, the dreams that come to us during our Heaven-world phase are wish-fulfilments. But they are something more than the idle gratification of fancy. They arise from the deep brooding of the mind upon its hopes and ideals. These may not seem to us very lofty, but they represent the phase of experience through which that particular soul is going in its evolution, and it may be necessary for that soul to go through the realisation of its hopes in order to profit by the lesson. The Muslim Heaven with its houri may not appeal to the Westerner, but it has been potent to send thousands of fanatical devotees to a sacrificial death in order that their faith might be spread among the infidels, and that faith has been a great force for good among tribes so primitive that they could not respond to a more sophisticated appeal. We must not judge another man's Heaven by our own standards. His Heaven is his wish-fulfilment, not ours. We must face the fact that the cat-burglar's Heaven would be full of easily climbed porches.

When we call back the spirits of the departed to tell us of their experiences in the Heaven-world whither they have gone, we are listening to the account of their dreams in the sleep of death. It is only when we are fortunate enough to get hold of one of the souls that are freed from the wheel of birth and death and are continuing their beneficent work for humanity upon the Inner Planes instead of entering into their rest, in other words, it is only when we get into touch with a Master, that we shall hear an account of the Heaven-world that shall give us a real understanding of its nature and the relation of its parts to the whole.

The account which is given by a person recently passed over is comparable to the account that is given of the working of a great hospital by one of the patients in its beds. He sees only a very small portion of the whole, and has no means of assessing its significance.

The account which is given by the guides, ministering spirit friends, and others whose task is to assist the departed, is equivalent to that which we might receive from the probationer nurses of the same hospital. It is not until we hear the doctors lecturing to the students that we begin to grasp the significance and scope of the great institution we are investigating.

Purgatory is a hospital for sick souls, where they are operated upon. The Heaven-world is first a convalescent home, and then a school. For some few it may also be a college. In the lower fields of Heaven, so often described in communications from the Inner Planes, souls rest and recuperate, dreaming pleasant dreams meanwhile that soothe them and make them happy. But this phase, having fulfiled its purpose, passes off and gives place to the next.

In order to understand the significance of these inter-incarnation phases, we must enter somewhat deeply into the philosophy of the subject. As we have already noted, heaven, and equally hell, are states of consciousness, not places. But if we realise the actual facts of the matter, we shall find that earth is also a state of consciousness. Modern physics is showing conclusively that matter is simply a form of force which, owing to the fact that it is in equilibrium, appears to us to be static. There is no such thing as dense matter as popularly understood. When you "bark your shins" over the coal-scuttle, you are really falling over electrical resistances. Incarnation is the state of consciousness which perceives these forms of force. Discarnation, or death, is the state of consciousness which no longer perceives them but has become subjective and is only aware of the content of its own consciousness. In death the gates of the senses are closed. Otherwise the man is unchanged. In fact we might say that viewed from the standpoint of the soul, death is simply the closing of the gates of the senses. If a man's consciousness is entirely limited to the five physical senses, though such men are rare, he is as much shut in with his own thoughts and as inaccessible as the sleeper lying oblivious upon a bed.

But does this sleep of death yield nothing but pleasant dreams and rest? No, it does much more than this. Any one who is familiar with the practice of mental work and meditation knows how powerful is the concentrated brooding of the mind upon some spiritual ideal. The highlands of heaven are the mounts of meditation. The soul, withdrawn from sense-impressions, is building thought-forms and giving itself auto-suggestion. These processes play an important part in formulating the vehicles of embodiment when the time comes for it to reincarnate.

The artist who dreams his dream of cosmic canvases is building faculty. On earth the realisation of his vision was limited by the skill of hand and eye. In the Heaven-world he is under no such limitations, and bodies forth his vision as he sees it. This trains faculty, and when he reincarnates, he will have gone some way towards building himself a physical vehicle in which hand and eye will cooperate with the inner vision and give it form. Life after life of effort, together with the intervening periods of meditation on the inner planes, gradually make the soul that which it wishes to be. If its wishes are unworthy or untrue, the regularly recurring spells of purgatory neutralise its efforts. Like Penelope's web, that which was woven by day is unpicked by night.

Those things which in our earth-life we have realised but failed to attain are achieved in heaven.

This subjective achievement builds faculty and we return to incarnation with the power to achieve latent in us. Life has done its work for us when it brings realisation, even if we are unable to achieve our realisations, for in the next life these will be within our grasp.

12
Communication With The Departed

The question of communication with the dead is a vexed one. Some people consider it entirely free from any element of harmfulness or even error, and feel it is not merely unnecessary but even blasphemous to "try the spirits whether they be of God." Others, and among these are many occultists, consider any attempt to communicate with the dead to be open to grave objection and harmful to both dead and living.

As in most other questions, the middle way between two extremes is the way of wisdom. Let us examine these two viewpoints and see where that middle way lies. Let us try to understand the factors involved in communication with the departed and consider the principles that should govern our relations with them, for we have relations with them whether we are consciously in communication with them or not. As long as they live in our memory there is a psychic rapport between us. As long as we feel any emotion about them, whether of love, grief, resentment, or fear, we are actively in touch with them; we are affecting them, and they are affecting us. We should therefore strive by all means in our power to achieve right relations with those who have passed over, and the most effectual way of achieving right relations is to possess accurate knowledge of inter-life conditions.

The person who has recently passed over is still in the same consciousness that he was upon the Earth plane. He awakes from the sleep of death into which he has been thrown by the Great Anaesthetist in exactly the same frame of mind as he was in prior to his passing. In this state he is readily accessible from the earth-plane. This condition soon fades, however, unless his memories be renewed and kept vivid by communications through a medium. Provided the disembodied soul is of normal and harmonious character, it does neither the dead nor the living any harm to exchange greetings during this phase of the discarnate period. In fact, if the departed soul has any unsolved problems upon his mind, or is anxious concerning his dear ones, it is of the greatest advantage to give him the opportunity of unburdening himself and completing any arrangements that he was unable to make before death came upon him. Souls sometimes cannot rest until they have done this, and remain in this intermediate state, anxiously trying to make themselves heard upon the earth-plane. To such souls a medium can be of the greatest service.

We must always remember, however, in dealing with the departed, that in a normal death-process this phase is comparatively brief, a matter of months at most, and that if we keep the attention of the disembodied soul focused upon the earth-plane by continually "calling him up" through a medium, he may fail to fall into the second sleep which heralds the second death. We may, in fact, cause him to develop astral insomnia and he will "walk," as the old phrase so expressively put it. It is possible for spirits to become earth-bound simply because they are kept from the astral sleep too long and adapt themselves to an intermediate condition instead of going on with the death processes and attaining to the next phase of the inter-life states.

Generally speaking, while it may be justifiable to it "get through" once or twice to those we love after they have passed over, it is inadvisable to keep on doing so because it is bad for both them and us. They, on their side, ought to be left in peace to get on with the tasks of their new life and to enter fully into its experiences; on our side, too, certain things have to be taken into consideration. Contact with the non-physical states of existence has a peculiar effect on the living, tending to draw them away from the plane of objective life and to dis-coordinate consciousness. This occurs even when the communicating entities are of the highest type, and it is well known by all who have had experience in the matter that precautions have to be taken to close the gates behind us each time we return after having issued forth from the house of flesh. People who are uninstructed in these matters do not understand either the necessity or the technique of these processes. The medium of high type, who is working under good guides, is looked after by the guides themselves, who see to the closing of the gates from their side of the Veil. But the sister who has no guides to protect her may go out from the seance room with her head whirling with the experiences she has been through, and if susceptible, may even be in a semi-psychic state herself. To clairvoyant sight she will appear surrounded by a host of beings who have been attracted to her sphere during the seance and who have not been dispersed at its closing. Trained psychics, be it noted, tend to forget their Inner Plane experiences as soon as the gates close behind them, and memory remains in abeyance until it is recalled by the concentration of thought once more upon the Inner Planes. It is very necessary to the health and stability of the psychic that he should be able to keep the planes of consciousness strictly separated, and this is one of the first things he learn to do when taught the technique of the Mysteries. The inexperienced sitter has no such technique and may have no one to advise her, and the consequences are apt to be unsatisfactory, or even disastrous. She becomes inco-ordinated and unsettled upon the physical plane, credulity growing with what it feeds upon, until the bounds of rational living are overpast and mental unbalance becomes apparent.

The question of research by trained investigators is upon a different footing; for the most part they are dealing with a different type of entity from those who come at the call of the bereaved. They are dealing with entities who are consciously and intelligently cooperating in the research, or who have come at the bidding of co-operating entities. Moreover the investigators, being experienced, know how to conduct their researches without injuring their communicators.

It is a natural impulse for those who have lost a loved one to rush to any source that holds out a hope of renewed contacts, but caution and discrimination are needed when so doing—it is not enough to obtain an evidential message, we must satisfy ourselves that we are obtaining it under conditions that will not injure either the dead nor the living, and these are conditions that have to be carefully observed with due regard to all the circumstances of the case and the temperament of the disembodied soul.

The Spiritualistic movement has rendered an incalculable service in bridging the gulf that used to separate the living from the dead. The fact of the survival of bodily death has been established beyond any possible question by any reasonable person who will take the trouble to acquaint himself with the evidence. If we want to do the best possible thing for those we love who have passed over, we will accept the fact of survival upon the basis of the evidence already available for us, and leave those we love to go on their way in peace. If all is not well with them, they themselves can take the necessary steps to get through to us. Let us leave the initiative with them. It is far better for all concerned not to call them back for any save the gravest reasons. But on the other hand, if a psychic spontaneously informs us that someone wishes to get in touch with us, and gives us clear evidence of the genuineness of the message, we should not hesitate to respond. But here again there is need of caution, human nature being what it is, for cases have been known of psychics who, whenever they hear of a death, take steps to get in touch with the relatives and induce them to "sit"—at so much a sitting!

13
The Pathologies Of Death–I

Hitherto in our studies we have been considering the normal course of death; but if we are to understand the nature of death and its problems, we must also consider what takes place if the processes of death do not run their normal course and the soul fails to obtain release from the bonds of matter and lingers unduly in an intermediate state.

The pathologies of the death-process can occur at two points: the state of mind of the person about to depart may be such as to prevent him from falling into the sleep of death; or having passed out safely, he may either refuse or be unable to pass on to the Second Death, and linger indefinitely in an intermediate state, becoming more and more abnormal as time goes on. There are a number of different forms of each of these pathologies, which we must consider in detail. The subject is a terrible one, but the best way to overcome fear is to face it, and we never know when we may be brought face to face with these problems. The understanding of their nature robs them of the superstitious terror with which they are invested in popular thought and brings them within the sphere of those things which we can face and deal with.

The spirit in which a person faces death is all important in determining the harmony or otherwise of the death-processes. Just as the unborn child "presents" at the Gates of Life the boney girdle of the pelvic arch and its birth is normal or abnormal according to the manner of its presentation, so does the outgoing soul "present" at the gates of death; and just as he should enter life head first, so should he go out of it with the higher levels of consciousness detached from earthly things and drawing the lower centres after them. For the lower consciousness to be forced out by the collapsing body before the higher consciousness has gained a foothold in the Unseen is a trying experience. Psychics frequently meet souls upon the Inner Planes who have gone through this experience, and they are invariably confused and distressed like lost dogs until they are enabled to make their adjustment and take hold upon the new life. A large proportion of the service that is given upon the Inner Planes is directed to "rounding up" these wandering souls and helping them to find their right place.

It is for this reason that the Church prays that we may be saved from sudden death, for the soul needs to make its preparations before withdrawing from the body. The soul of the man who is killed instantaneously, or who dies without recovering consciousness, has certain difficulties to overcome which do not beset the person who dies naturally and gradually. There are those upon the Inner Planes, however, whose work it is to deal with innocent souls thus flung violently out of life, and to minimise their distress; psychics tell us that these Watchers hover like hawks in the Hither Hereafter watching for outcoming souls, and going on swift wing to those who show any sign of distress. It is rare that souls come out into the next life who have not got some friend who has already passed over to welcome them; but if they have to be ejected violently, as it were, from the plane of earth, and are thrust out backwards, struggling and resisting, their faces are turned towards the plane which they have left, and they cannot be induced to turn round and look towards the plane upon which they are entering. It is a case of malpresentation upon the plane of death, and skilled care is needed to restore normality.

The man who fears death greatly is liable thus to "malpresent," and he is born into the next life with suffering, difficulty, and danger. If he fights up to his last breath, the Great Anaesthetist may be unable to get in his merciful work, and that soul goes through the death process in full consciousness. Such souls generally fail to realise that they have died. They are accustomed to look upon death as synonymous with the extinction of consciousness, and if they find that they have not lost consciousness, and still retain, in their own imagination at any rate, the same body they have always had, though devoid of sensation or weight, it takes some persuasion to convince them that they have passed through the Gates of Death and are disembodied. They see themselves still as having their accustomed form, and they cannot be made to realise that it is only a thought-form in their own imagination, and that nobody else can see it unless he is psychic. They naturally associate this form with their familiar haunts, and because they think of themselves as being there, ipso facto, they are there, and can be perceived by psychics and sensed by any of their friends who are at all sensitive, often with very unfortunate results. The person who sees death coming, however, knows what to expect, and when he wakes from the sleep of death he is prepared to find himself without his physical body and so has no difficulty in making his adjustment. In fact, people who have been to the very verge of death and returned again have often reported that when they recovered consciousness they were amazed to find that they were alive, and at first could not be convinced that they had not died.

The dead man who does not know he is dead naturally receives a shock when he finds that he is impalpable to those with whom he expects to be able to get into touch. He speaks to the watchers at the bedside, and they do not answer him. He stretches out a hand to touch them and attract their attention, and it passes right through the shoulder upon which he would lay it. To him, they are ghosts, and he is overwhelmed with bewilderment. He wanders from place to place of his familiar haunts, seeking to accost those he knows, but they turn a deaf ear to him. Presently, however, he may find one who, being psychic, may be aware of his presence.

Now we come to an important question, especially important for the readers of these pages, who being interested in these subjects and giving them their attention, are generally in possession of some degree at least of awareness of the Unseen, often in fact, of more than they realise. They have got to be extremely careful how they deal with the panic-stricken disembodied soul, or they may find themselves in the same situation as the would-be rescuer of the drowning. The wisest thing they can do, unless they are experienced psychics, is to refuse to attempt a rescue for which they are ill-equipped, and to go quickly to fetch help, asking the services of some person or group with the necessary knowledge who will take the wandering soul in hand and help him to adjust himself and go on with death's journey into the fuller light. For remember this, once a soul has crossed the Great Divide, the way of light lies ahead, not behind; the one thing to do is to thrust him off from the earth-plane and by all means in our power to prevent him from obtaining a foothold upon that dark and slippery shore that leads down to the waters of Lethe. Make him turn round and swim to the other bank whether he likes it or not; it is the kindest thing to do, however he may cry out against it, and the swim is well within his powers if he will but try. With each stroke that takes him away from the dark shore of Death-in-Life he is nearer to the Life-after-Death. He is struggling from darkness to dawn, and the way becomes brighter as he advances. Do not let us fear the dead when they come to us, but do not let us allow a panic-stricken disembodied entity to clutch us round the neck, like a drowning man, in its efforts to remain on the plane of form. The cowardice of a departed soul may evoke our pity, but it cannot command our sympathy and we ought not to pander to it. To do so is not to help him, but to condemn him to a terrible fate, the fate of the Earth-bound.

At all costs he must be made to let go his hold on the plane of form and induced to set out upon his journey to the Great Light which shall enlighten even his darkened consciousness.

The man who dies an accidental death, passing suddenly out of life in the full possession of his faculties, is usually dazed but not distressed, because death has come so quickly. He feels nothing and his mind is more or less a blank, or working very slowly and disconnectedly. The newspapers often remark upon the extraordinary fortitude of those who have been severely injured in an accident; anyone who has ever been in an accident knows that the shock is its own anaesthetic, and the pain and collapse do not come till later. Often they do not know they are injured till someone draws their attention to it. The severity of the injury is invariably in inverse ratio to the screaming.

In some cases of head injury a person will linger for days, or even weeks before finally passing out. In such cases they are for the most part as deeply unconscious upon the Inner Planes as they are upon the physical plane, but towards the end of the time, when the body is getting ready to set the soul free, there may be brief periods of dream in which they glimpse the Inner Planes more or less dimly. In such a case the outgoing soul can be greatly helped by the rites of the dying, even if unconscious, and there should be prayer, at the bedside if possible, even when there is deep unconsciousness, and this should be kept up until they breathe their last. If unable to be present at the bedside in the flesh, imagine yourself to be there, and you will be present in the spirit, and the outgoing soul, waking to psychic consciousness, will see you, even if the bystanders do not. A great deal of help can be given in this way, and the soul is prepared subconsciously for departure even when there can be no conscious preparation.

14
The Pathologies Of Death–II

Intense fear, as we have already seen, prevents the soul from falling into the sleep of death and going through the death processes in a normal and harmonious manner. We must bear in mind however, that there are two kinds of fear: the fear of the person who will not go to meet death as he should when his time comes, and the fear of the person who is being attacked. In the latter case, the fear is not of death, but of the attacker. Souls thus thrust violently out of life are kept from the sleep of death by their fear, even as are the others, and do not realise that they are disembodied, nor that they have passed beyond the reach of their attacker. For a time there is terror and confusion, but that is soon allayed by the services of the Invisible Helpers. We have no need to be anxious for the welfare of the souls of the innocent victims of violence. They pass on to their own place and are speedily soothed and restored to normal.

The thought-form of their fear, however, is another matter, and this may remain at the place where the crime occurred as an exceedingly vivid image in the thought-atmosphere of the spot. If anyone comes there in whom the etheric double is loosely knit so that he has some capacity as a materialising medium, the thought-form may even take on a shadowy shape and the sounds of the struggle be heard again. Let it be clearly realised, however, that the unfortunate victim of a crime is not earth-bound and compelled to haunt the spot of his murder, it is only the mental image formulated by both murderer and victim which remains. No one is suffering; it is alarming and unpleasant but not dangerous, and can be readily dispersed by the use of the appropriate methods, some of which, suitable for use by persons who are not trained occultists, I have given in my book "Psychic Self-defence."

The practice of holding a service on the spot where a violent death took place is also of the greatest value, for it breaks up any thought-forms that may have been left behind in the reflecting ether. Firstly, it enables thought to be concentrated for meditation much more effectually than can be done if there is no focussing-point for the mind to centre upon. Secondly, it enables the meditations of several persons to be synchronised, thus greatly reinforcing the effect of their work. At times of emotional tension and shock it is not easy to concentrate the mind and break out of the circling train of sad thoughts ever returning upon itself, but the mind can follow a form of words that is set before it at a time when it would be quite incapable of formulating any meditation of its own.

The following little service may be found helpful in bringing rest to the soul of one who has passed out of life suddenly and unprepared, and of easing and reconciling the hearts of those left behind. Even if there be none to assist in the performance of the ceremony, it should nevertheless be read aloud, with the appropriate actions as instructed. It is not nearly so effectual if performed silently.

If it is not possible to perform the ceremony at the scene of the tragedy, let something intimately associated with the deceased be held in the hand of whoever takes the part of celebrant.

The ritual can be performed by a single person, but it is more beautiful and effectual if performed by two, the one reinforcing the other. In our terminology, they are called the ministrant and lector.

Ritual For The Peace Of The Soul That Has Passed Out By A Sudden Or Violent Death

Ministrant: At eventide it shall be light.

Lector: The Lord is my light and my salvation, whom shall I fear? The Lord is the strength of my life, of whom shall I be afraid ? Though an host should encamp against me, my heart shall not fear; though war should arise against me, in this will I be content. I had fainted unless I had believed to see the goodness of the Lord in the Land of the Ever-living. Wait upon the Lord, be of good courage, and He shall strengthen thy heart. Wait, I say, upon the Lord.

Hymn 193 Hymns A.& M. "Jesu, lover of my soul."

Ministrant: (kneeling)

All-loving and heavenly Father, look down upon our grief for one (those) taken suddenly from us in the midst of life, and strengthen us that we may have courage and confidence in Thine unfailing mercy.

All: Amen.

Ministrant: (Raising right hand as in calling attention, and pressing to his breast the relic of the departed held in the left hand). Let us now summon our friend (gives fullname) to join in our service, with us adoring the All-merciful Father of us all.

(All present visualise the deceased standing
facing the ministrant.)

Ministrant: Let us pray.

All: (kneeling, and visualising the deceased kneeling with
them).

Jesus, son of Mary, have mercy upon us. Christ, son
of God, have mercy upon us. Jesus, son of Mary, have
mercy upon us.

Ministrant: O Master Jesus, Lord of love and compassion, who
didst descend into the place of death and preach to
the spirits in prison, take, we beseech Thee, the soul
of our dear one into Thy loving care. O Thou good
shepherd, seek that which is lost, and bring the
wandering soul safe into Thy fold.

All: Amen.

Ministrant: Let us all join in the Lord's Prayer.

All: Our Father . . .

Lector: Jesus saith: "Come unto me all ye that labour and are
heavy laden, and I will give you rest." Verily, verily I
say unto you, the hour is coming, and now is, when
the dead shall hear the voice of the Son of God, and
they that hear shall live. The people that sat in
darkness saw a great light, and to them that sat in the
region and shadow of death, light is sprung up.

Ministrant: O Father of Lights, in whom is no darkness nor shadow of turning, send, we beseech Thee, the angels of Thy Presence to minister to our beloved one, who passed through the gates of death unprepared, that he may not wander as a sheep lost upon the mountains, but be gathered safely into the fold of Thy Son our Saviour, Jesus Christ.

All:	Amen.

Hymn 223 (A. & M.) "Hark, hark, my soul, angelic songs are swelling."

Ministrant: (kneeling)
Lord, now suffer Thou Thy servant to depart in peace, according to Thy word, that he may enter into Thy rest until it shall please Thee to bid him go forth again in Thy service.

All:	Amen.

Ministrant: (rising and making the Sign of the Cross over the place where the deceased has been visualised as standing). Depart in peace, beloved friend, marked with the Sign of Christ.

Hymn 300 (A. & M.) "All hail the power of Jesus Name."

Ministrant: Let the peace of God be upon us all till the day dawn and the shadows flee away.

All:	Amen.

There are certain points to be observed if this ceremony is to be magically efficacious. Firstly there must be some link with the departed, and this link can be of various forms. It may be the link of place, when the ceremony is performed at the site of the tragedy; or it may be the link of time when it is performed on the anniversary of the tragedy; or it may be what is known to occultists as a magnetic link, that is to say, some object intimately associated with the departed, which is charged with his magnetism, and which has not been handled by other people since he used it last. The most efficacious method is to employ at least two of these links simultaneously.

All who take part in the ceremony should visualise the departed as standing on a particular spot, and imagine him entering into the ritual of the service, kneeling when they kneel and praying with them. This builds up a thought-form which provides a point of contact with the departed spirit. It is not designed to procure a materialisation, for this would be undesirable, but it is essential to the efficacy of the operation to obtain the presence of the departed; the visualisation of his physical form and the simultaneous calling of his name is the readiest way, of doing this.

This method should only be used when it is desired to get in touch with a departed soul, which may be wandering on the astral plane, in order to enable it to pass onward upon its journey and complete the process of departure which the violent and unprepared death may have disorganised. To employ it to induce the departed soul to return again and again to comfort us in our affliction is unjustifiable, for it is very harmful to the soul to be thus held to the earthsphere. His condition may be likened to that of a man who has attempted to leap across a stream and has missed his footing and fallen into the mud and reeds of the nearer bank. We call to him, attract his attention, and reach him a hand and pull him back to shore again; but we only do this in order that we may be able to give him a fresh start. If, having grasped his hand, we cling to it, we should thwart his purpose. Once he has been enabled to gather himself together upon firm ground, he is able to take a run and leap, and this time he should land safely on the further bank.

It must be clearly realised that the dead man, once he has quilted his house of flesh, must at all costs go on and complete his journey before the night of the soul overtakes him. If we delay him unduly by constantly recalling him to contact with the earth-plane, we expose him to the worst evil that can possibly befall him, the state which, by occultists is called Death-in-Life and by spiritualists, earth-bound.

Normally, if left to its own devices, the soul will eventually succeed in reaching the further bank, but it is in our power to help greatly in that process in the way indicated.

15
How The Adept Meets Death

I t is a maxim of the Path that those who have overcome are known by their serenity; the Adept dies, as he has lived, serenely. Death has no terrors for the man who knows the actuality of re-incarnation through his own memories of past lives. He has died many times before and the process is familiar to him. He is accustomed daily to withdraw consciousness from the brain and enter into the Higher Self in meditation. He knows that the time has now come to go out through that familiar gate and close it behind him, returning not again. Through long years of discipline upon the Path to adepthood he has been laying up treasure in heaven; he is accustomed to think of himself as a spirit, not as a physical body; for him the body is but an observation-post which he has constructed for himself upon the plane of earth.

He knows that the call to withdraw has come to him for one of two reasons; his physical body may be no longer a serviceable machine, and it is better and cheaper to scrap it and get a new one than to patch up that which is past repair. Or it may be that he has completed his task upon earth and is summoned to go up higher. He accepts death freely and without cavilling, for he knows that if it were not his Master's command that called him forth, all the powers of Death and Hell could not prevail to drive him out of his habitation of flesh.

As he awaits the processes of the body that shall open the gates to him, he sinks deeper into meditation, seeking to distil the essence of life's experiences; observing the lessons it has set him, noting those he has learnt and those which are as yet imperfectly acquired, and striving by intensive effort to complete his realisation of those lessons before the time comes for his departure. Soon he will know whether he has completed his task or whether he is destined to return to earth again to finish his work.

If he finds that earth-life is not yet finished for him and that he is to return, he will bend his energies to the task of constructing the archetype of the etheric mould which is to give form to his body and direction to his destiny when he comes once more to earth; he endeavours to engrave upon the seed-atom the memory of the Mysteries wherein he has been initiated, thereby surrounding it with those "trailing clouds of glory" with which, the initiate soul is invested when it passes out once more through those gates which when seen from above are the gates of birth and when seen from below are the Gates of Death.

Clearly and persistently he formulates his ideal so that his soul, when it goes forth, shall be directed towards its goal and not wander aimlessly in the other world. He knows that within a cycle of three lives he has complete free will. If this life has borne the fruits of past endeavour, then he may count with reasonable certainty upon the next life seeing the achievement of his aim. As soon as he finds that his grip upon this life is loosening, the adept is preparing for the next life.

For the adept, there is no parting from those he loves; he has long learnt to love the spiritual essence of each soul, and the loosening of the silver cord and the breaking of the golden bowl mean to him the casting down of the barriers that separate him from perfect union with that which he loves in each one of those dear to him.

Which is best, to be in physical touch with those whose souls are remote from us through lack of sympathy, or to be in a spiritual union of perfect sympathy and understanding with the real, the immortal and indestructible Higher Self of one dear to us? The former is the real separation, not the latter. Those who have the higher consciousness can commune together independently of the body while they are still in this earth-life, and death only increases their faculty of communication. They are far closer to each other spiritually when there are no longer any barriers erected by the limitations of the body.

When the time comes for the adept to set forth, he summons to him those who are dearest that they may ease his parting and companion him upon the first stages of his journey. Those who can come in the flesh gather about him; those who cannot, come thither in the astral projection; and those who have gone on ahead through the great Gates are summoned also that they may return and await him upon the threshold.

The Magic Circle is drawn about him, sealed at the four quadrants with the Names of the four mighty Archangels, and candles burn at head and foot. All sit silent in meditation while the dying man treads once more the Path of withdrawing, the path of symbol-vision that he has trodden so often when rising on the planes. As he withdraws, the Gates swing softly for his passage, and those who are watching see in the spirit-vision the coming of a Mighty One to meet him, the Archangel of his Order; a light shines about the bed like the last ray of the setting sun darting from under a cloud, clearly visible even to the physical eye, and the soul of the adept is gone.

It is the promise of the Mysteries to their initiates that they shall go through the Gates of Death in full consciousness and be met by the Great Initiator; it is also the privilege of those of his brethren who companion the initiate upon his last journey that they, too, shall stand upon the threshold and look beyond into the hereafter and see for themselves the path they will follow when their time comes.

About The Author

Dion Fortune (1891–1946), founder of The Society of Inner Light, is recognized as one of the most luminous and significant figures of 20th-century esoteric thought. A prolific writer, pioneer psychologist, and powerful psychic, she dedicated her life to the revival of the Mystery Tradition of the West. She left behind a solidly established system of teaching and a school of initiation based on her knowledge of many systems, ancient and modern. Her books were published before World War II, and have been continuously in demand since that time.

To Our Readers

Weiser Books, an imprint of Red Wheel/Weiser, publishes books across the entire spectrum of occult and esoteric subjects. Our mission is to publish quality books that will make a difference in people's lives without advocating any one particular path or field of study. We value the integrity, originality, and depth of knowledge of our authors.

Our readers are our most important resource, and we appreciate your input, suggestions, and ideas about what you would like to see published. Please feel free to contact us, to request our latest book catalog, or to be added to our mailing list.

Red Wheel/Weiser, LLC
P.O. Box 612
York Beach, ME 03910-0612
www.redwheelweiser.com